DARE TO BE YOURSELF

QUOTES AND AFFIRMATIONS

LYNETTE DIEHM

DARE TO BE YOU MEDIA

COPYRIGHT

Copyright © 2023 Dare To Be You Pty Ltd\ Lynette Diehm. All rights reserved. No part of this book may be used or reproduced by any means, electronic, or mechanical, including photocopying, recording, taping or by any information storage retrieval system without the written permission of the author except in the case of brief quotations embodied in critical articles and reviews.

Because of the dynamic nature of the Internet, any web addresses or links in this book may have changed since publication and may no longer be valid.

Other books by Lynette Diehm

Dare To Be You: Break free from the shackles of the past to become Yourself, Outstanding and Unstoppable!

Dare To Be Outstanding in Life: Quotes & Affirmations

Dare To Be Unstoppable with Relationships: Quotes & Affirmations

Dare To Be You: Gratitude Diary

Turn your anxiety into a weapon that fuels and excites you, by turning your negative thoughts about the unknown into positive thoughts about possibilities and opportunities.

Dare To Be YOU, Yourself, Outstanding and Unstoppable Today!

Yourself

You are not your past.
You are not your future.
You are not your job or job title.
You are not the role you play in society.
You are only the person you are being in the here and now (present).

Dare To Be YOU, Yourself, Outstanding and Unstoppable Today!

Yourself

In the midst of uncertain times, always remember who you are, what you stand for, and that strength and stability come from within you.
So, always believe in yourself, as that is how genuine miracles will manifest.

Dare To Be YOU, Yourself, Outstanding and Unstoppable Today!

Yourself

You are worthy and deserve really amazing two sided friendships. If someone is constantly texting you negative judgemental messages, then it's time to walk away as continuing the friendship will only hurt you more.

Dare To Be YOU, Yourself, Outstanding and Unstoppable Today!

Yourself

What's better for you? A life full of regret letting fear rule your life and never trying new things. Or one where you give everything a go as you see what you are capable of, where you are reaching your potential.

Dare To Be YOU, Yourself, Outstanding and Unstoppable Today!

Yourself

There is abundance all around if you choose to see it. You just need to open your eyes and take a good look around to see it.

Dare To Be YOU, Yourself, Outstanding and Unstoppable Today!

Yourself

Remember, there are always going to be people that, no matter who you are or what you do, feel insecure around you and threatened by you in life. Continue to be your amazing self. Don't stoop to their level.

Dare To Be YOU, Yourself, Outstanding and Unstoppable Today!

Yourself

To love yourself is always being honest with yourself and keeping the promises you make to yourself.

Dare To Be YOU, Yourself, Outstanding and Unstoppable Today!

Yourself

Doing personal and professional development will put you ahead of the market for roles and also assist you in overcoming your insecurities.

Dare To Be YOU, Yourself, Outstanding and Unstoppable Today!

Yourself

You are allowed to be an amazing person and totally awesome at what you do. You do not need anyone else's approval to be amazing!

Dare To Be YOU, Yourself, Outstanding and Unstoppable Today!

Yourself

Don't stoop to the level of those that say or do something against you.
You are better than that. Keep your standards and expectations high and know it is their story, not yours.
Emotionally distance yourself from the situation.

Dare To Be YOU, Yourself, Outstanding and Unstoppable Today!

Yourself

Life changes so fast.
If you blink an eye, you will miss it and the many miracles that life brings with it.
Always be grateful for what you have and the many miracles yet to come.

Dare To Be YOU, Yourself, Outstanding and Unstoppable Today!

Yourself

Your belief in yourself and in what you are capable of is what makes everything possible. Don't let others tarnish your belief in yourself.

Dare To Be YOU, Yourself, Outstanding and Unstoppable Today!

Yourself

Ask yourself how important it is to you.
If it is important enough to you, no matter what, you will always achieve it.

Dare To Be YOU, Yourself, Outstanding and Unstoppable Today!

Yourself

Trust the universe has your back and the universe will have your back.
Trust and belief go a very long way!

Dare To Be YOU, Yourself, Outstanding and Unstoppable Today!

Yourself

Being amazing isn't about what you can or can't do. It's more about the person you are being around others.

Dare To Be YOU, Yourself, Outstanding and Unstoppable Today!

Yourself

If you want to be successful in what you're doing, be sure to focus your energy on what motivates you to achieve that success, as that will drive you towards your success.

Dare To Be YOU, Yourself, Outstanding and Unstoppable Today!

Yourself

Being happy and positive is a choice.
Choose wisely your thoughts, words and actions.

Dare To Be YOU, Yourself, Outstanding and Unstoppable Today!

Yourself

When you truly become at peace with who you are, you will have no limitations, no matter what.
Because you can do and achieve everything!

Dare To Be YOU, Yourself, Outstanding and Unstoppable Today!

Yourself

A smile will always brighten someone's day.
So smile today and see whose day you can brighten up.

Dare To Be YOU, Yourself, Outstanding and Unstoppable Today!

Yourself

Having good health isn't just about what you eat or your exercise routine.
It's also about what you say, think, feel and do.
A holistic view is best when it comes to your health.

Dare To Be YOU, Yourself, Outstanding and Unstoppable Today!

Yourself

When you stand true to your values and self-worth, wonderful things happen in your life.

Dare To Be YOU, Yourself, Outstanding and Unstoppable Today!

Yourself

When you go looking for it you will never find it.
When you stop looking and least expect it you will find it!

Dare To Be YOU, Yourself, Outstanding and Unstoppable Today!

Yourself

Knowing when to walk away from emotionally immature family members, when they continually hurt, you will save your life.

Dare To Be YOU, Yourself, Outstanding and Unstoppable Today!

Yourself

Learning to be your true self is one of the most rewarding but hardest things you will ever do. There will always be external influences put in the way of testing your convictions. Stand true and strong.

Dare To Be YOU, Yourself, Outstanding and Unstoppable Today!

Yourself

It is important to take responsibility for your life, your thoughts, your actions and words, as they are the things that will change your life. Giving it meaning, purpose, and value.

Dare To Be YOU, Yourself, Outstanding and Unstoppable Today!

Yourself

Reaching for the stars will stretch you, but if you have a simple plan of action and you take action, you will get there.

Dare To Be YOU, Yourself, Outstanding and Unstoppable Today!

Yourself

Confidence isn't in the person you are on the outside. When you realize just how amazing you really are on the inside, that confidence will shine through on the outside.

Dare To Be YOU, Yourself, Outstanding and Unstoppable Today!

Yourself

Self-belief and self-love are the two most powerful things on the planet.
Once you have these two things, you can, with a little discipline, reach the stars.

Dare To Be YOU, Yourself, Outstanding and Unstoppable Today!

Yourself

When faced with a challenge in life, remember that you are strong enough.
The universe doesn't put in front of you anything you can't handle.

Dare To Be YOU, Yourself, Outstanding and Unstoppable Today!

Yourself

Change your approach and do things differently when applying for jobs.
This shows the employer who you are and where your head is at.
Personal and professional development work together to build on your value in the workplace.

Dare To Be YOU, Yourself, Outstanding and Unstoppable Today!

Yourself

Knowledge gives you power, so never stop learning because the moment you do, you lose that power.
Remember to use that power wisely.

Dare To Be YOU, Yourself, Outstanding and Unstoppable Today!

Yourself

You only get one life, so laugh, love, and forgive as much as possible.

Dare To Be YOU, Yourself, Outstanding and Unstoppable Today!

Yourself

Putting yourself and your needs first isn't selfish or easy. Do it so that you can honour who you are.

Dare To Be YOU, Yourself, Outstanding and Unstoppable Today!

Yourself

Being your true and authentic self in life is very important. You must not let other people pollute that purity.

Dare To Be YOU, Yourself, Outstanding and Unstoppable Today!

Yourself

When people try to put you down, ignore them, as it has nothing to do with you and everything to do with what is inside them.

Dare To Be YOU, Yourself, Outstanding and Unstoppable Today!

Yourself

Part of your uniqueness are the talents you have. To show your individuality, share your best talents with the world!

Dare To Be YOU, Yourself, Outstanding and Unstoppable Today!

Yourself

The themes you have going on in your life tell a story about who you are and how you see the world.
The best themes in your life are yet to come!

Dare To Be YOU, Yourself, Outstanding and Unstoppable Today!

Yourself

Letting go of the past and working towards your future is not selfish as you can help others along the way to realise their true potential!

Dare To Be YOU, Yourself, Outstanding and Unstoppable Today!

Yourself

Serving others isn't about getting rewards back from doing things for others.
It is about using the best parts of yourself and selflessly helping others without a want or need to be rewarded.

Dare To Be YOU, Yourself, Outstanding and Unstoppable Today!

Yourself

When you truly become at peace with whom you are, you will have no limitations on what you can do and achieve in your life.

Dare To Be YOU, Yourself, Outstanding and Unstoppable Today!

Yourself

When you have a mindset for success, you are constantly working on your internal world.

Dare To Be YOU, Yourself, Outstanding and Unstoppable Today!

Yourself

The biggest investment you should ever make is the one in yourself and your own personal and professional growth.

Dare To Be YOU, Yourself, Outstanding and Unstoppable Today!

Yourself

Now more than ever, it's important to know who you are and what makes you happy. You only get one life, so focus your energy on the end goal/game, which should ultimately be your happiness.

Dare To Be YOU, Yourself, Outstanding and Unstoppable Today!

Yourself

Life is full of peaks and valleys, swings and roundabouts. What matters the most is how you handle them and bounce back from the low lows.

Dare To Be YOU, Yourself, Outstanding and Unstoppable Today!

Yourself

People come and people go, but the only person who will stay in your life no matter what, for the duration of your life, is you.

Dare To Be YOU, Yourself, Outstanding and Unstoppable Today!

Yourself

You are not your job; you are not the role you play in society; you are not the role you play in your family; you are not what you study. You are a genuine person with feelings, a personality, likes, and dislikes. So, dig deep to find out who you really are and be that wonderful person because you are amazing!

Dare To Be YOU, Yourself, Outstanding and Unstoppable Today!

Yourself

When life knocks you down, always remember to roll forwards, figure out the lessons you need to learn. Learn those lessons, adjust your course & continue forwards. Never let bad things & people keep you down. Surround yourself with people who love, respect, and support you.

Dare To Be YOU, Yourself, Outstanding and Unstoppable Today!

Yourself

Now is the time to stop hiding in the shadows behind the mask and take them off to show the world all sides of you. You have within you that which empowers & inspires others to be all that they can be, by embracing their true & authentic selves as the power is within.

Dare To Be YOU, Yourself, Outstanding and Unstoppable Today!

Yourself

The most important mastery you will ever need in life is that of self mastery.
Mastering your thoughts, emotions, actions, and reactions to what is going on around you is what will make or break you in life.

Dare To Be YOU, Yourself, Outstanding and Unstoppable Today!

Yourself

Your past is not a life sentence, so never be afraid or feel as though you are trapped by it because you are not.
The only prison you are trapped in is your mind.

Dare To Be YOU, Yourself, Outstanding and Unstoppable Today!

Yourself

When you believe in miracles, anything is possible.
So never give that power away.

Dare To Be YOU, Yourself, Outstanding and Unstoppable Today!

Yourself

When you believe in miracles,
anything is possible.
So never give that power
away.

Dare To Be YOU, Yourself,
Outstanding and Unstoppable
Today!

Yourself

Remember that when you love what you do, you also share that love with others. Do what you love and love what you do always.

Dare To Be YOU, Yourself, Outstanding and Unstoppable Today!

Yourself

Don't worry if sometimes other people's feathers get ruffled. That's just Life! We are here on earth to live our lives by being true to ourselves and not being what other people want us to be.

Dare To Be YOU, Yourself, Outstanding and Unstoppable Today!

Yourself

I am who I am; I love who I am; I know who I am; I know what I want.
I will never apologize for putting myself and my needs first, as it's my life and my life alone to live.

Dare To Be YOU, Yourself, Outstanding and Unstoppable Today!

Yourself

Some people feel peace, joy, love, and positivity.
Other people feel anger, bitterness, hatred, spite and un–forgiveness.
We all have a choice on what we feel, so which do you choose?

Dare To Be YOU, Yourself, Outstanding and Unstoppable Today!

Yourself

We are raised in a society where striving for perfection is everything.
From having the perfect body, looks, partner, relationship, family, job, home, & car.
If we aren't perfect, then we are socially not accepted in society, causing emotional/mental illness & alienates those who are treated like outcasts.
We should strive to be uniquely & individually different, embracing our individuality, loving each other & ourselves for how wonderfully different, unique & amazing we are.

Dare To Be YOU, Yourself, Outstanding and Unstoppable Today!

Yourself

I am the hero in my story and intend to be amazing at it in life.

Dare To Be YOU, Yourself, Outstanding and Unstoppable Today!

Yourself

It is okay to have more than one passion for what you want to do in life.
People chop and change careers all the time.
There are no rules for your happiness.

Dare To Be YOU, Yourself, Outstanding and Unstoppable Today!

Yourself

Do the job to the best of your ability, but remember to take breaks and don't push yourself into burning out. Be gentle with yourself.

Dare To Be YOU, Yourself, Outstanding and Unstoppable Today!

Yourself

Surround yourself with like-minded people.
Leave the dramatic fair-weather friends behind you as they no longer fit in your life.
Just let them go.

Dare To Be YOU, Yourself, Outstanding and Unstoppable Today!

Yourself

Put a little piece of your soul
into everything that you do
and you will find you will
enjoy life more.

Dare To Be YOU, Yourself,
Outstanding and Unstoppable
Today!

Yourself

I am no longer hiding my true self from others, by hiding behind a mask and pretending to be what everyone else wants me to be, for their approvals. The only approval I need is my own.

Dare To Be YOU, Yourself, Outstanding and Unstoppable Today!

Yourself

I choose to be courageously daring in all my endeavors as I come across challenges that stretch and push me outside my comfort zone.

Dare To Be YOU, Yourself, Outstanding and Unstoppable Today!

Yourself

Share with the intention of sharing and informing others and not to get something back.
Be generous and kind!

Dare To Be YOU, Yourself, Outstanding and Unstoppable Today!

Yourself

Stay calm and focused on everything you do, so that you can think clearly and do your best.

Dare To Be YOU, Yourself, Outstanding and Unstoppable Today!

Yourself

Never stick with something because you think it is your only option. Speak to others and find out what all the options are, then make an informed decision.

Dare To Be YOU, Yourself, Outstanding and Unstoppable Today!

Yourself

Teach yourself to respond instead of reacting to things, and life will get easier. Roll with the waves and not against them in the storm.

Dare To Be YOU, Yourself, Outstanding and Unstoppable Today!

Yourself

Be quietly confident and
not loudly insecure.

**Dare To Be YOU, Yourself,
Outstanding and Unstoppable
Today!**

Yourself

Show a little patience and kindness in all that you do. Too often we get angry and jump to conclusions when something we want doesn't go our way.

Dare To Be YOU, Yourself, Outstanding and Unstoppable Today!

Yourself

Be patient and let the universe do its best to move things along for you.

Dare To Be YOU, Yourself, Outstanding and Unstoppable Today!

Yourself

Stay positive in the eye of
the storm and know that it,
too, will pass.

Dare To Be YOU, Yourself,
Outstanding and Unstoppable
Today!

Yourself

Turn your anxiety into a weapon that fuels and excites you by turning your negative thoughts about the unknown into positive thoughts about possibilities and opportunities.

Dare To Be YOU, Yourself, Outstanding and Unstoppable Today!

Yourself

Being authentically healthy
in mind, body and spirit
means that you are always
true to and putting yourself
first, no matter what.

Dare To Be YOU, Yourself,
Outstanding and Unstoppable
Today!

Yourself

Now more than ever, it's important to know who you are and what makes you happy.
You only get one life.
So, focus your energy on the end goal/game, which should ultimately be your happiness.

Dare To Be YOU, Yourself, Outstanding and Unstoppable Today!

Yourself

To love is a part of life. You can't possibly experience the true power of love and loving others if you don't love yourself.

Dare To Be YOU, Yourself, Outstanding and Unstoppable Today!

Yourself

When someone undermines you, rise above it.
There's no need to stoop to their level to prove them wrong.
You are better than that.

Dare To Be YOU, Yourself, Outstanding and Unstoppable Today!

Yourself

When life gets tough, you need to be even tougher and push through until you get to your final destination.

Dare To Be YOU, Yourself, Outstanding and Unstoppable Today!

Yourself

We are powerful beyond our wildest dreams, as touching the heart of just one person can end up moving the hearts of millions of people in life.

Dare To Be YOU, Yourself, Outstanding and Unstoppable Today!

Yourself

Nothing worthwhile in life is ever easy, so keep going, find your way around the roadblocks and move through the overgrown weeds.
You will get to the light at the end of the tunnel.

Dare To Be YOU, Yourself, Outstanding and Unstoppable Today!

Yourself

Everything we do in life is a choice.
So I choose to be amazing, happy and abundant now.

Dare To Be YOU, Yourself, Outstanding and Unstoppable Today!

Yourself

True and lasting transformation comes from within.
The only way to have long-lasting change in your life is to start from within yourself.

Dare To Be YOU, Yourself, Outstanding and Unstoppable Today!

Yourself

Teach others how you want them to treat you.
Never accept treatment below what you think you are worthy of.

Dare To Be YOU, Yourself, Outstanding and Unstoppable Today!

Yourself

Sometimes life gets in the way is a great excuse for why you didn't do something.
How about you just keep your promises to yourself!

Dare To Be YOU, Yourself, Outstanding and Unstoppable Today!

Yourself

People come and people go, but the only person who will stay in your life no matter what, for the duration of your life, is you.

Dare To Be YOU, Yourself, Outstanding and Unstoppable Today!

Yourself

Don't be trapped, but empowered by your past, as it will set you free.

Dare To Be YOU, Yourself, Outstanding and Unstoppable Today!

Yourself

We learn and grow from our mistakes.
We would be like a machine if we did not make mistakes.
Mistakes are a natural part of evolution.

Dare To Be YOU, Yourself, Outstanding and Unstoppable Today!

Yourself

I am confident,
I am driven,
I am focused
I am unstoppable.
I've got what it takes!
This is fun,
This is easy
I've got this!

Dare To Be YOU, Yourself,
Outstanding and Unstoppable
Today!

Yourself

Sometimes silence is all it takes to show people where you are at with things. Silence isn't necessarily agreeing, it is a part of knowing what battles to fight in life.

Dare To Be YOU, Yourself, Outstanding and Unstoppable Today!

Yourself

Without uncertainty, you will have no growth, as you will always be stuck in your comfort zone.
Uncertainty brings challenge, curiosity, learning and growth.

Dare To Be YOU, Yourself, Outstanding and Unstoppable Today!

Yourself

When you are too hard on yourself, you can be your own worst enemy so, ease up on yourself a little and see how much better life becomes.

Dare To Be YOU, Yourself, Outstanding and Unstoppable Today!

Yourself

Being your true self is a necessary choice.
If you choose not to show people who you really are, one day, you will be found out.

Dare To Be YOU, Yourself, Outstanding and Unstoppable Today!

Yourself

You are the captain of your own ship whether you sail on to the next dock is up to you and no one else.

Dare To Be YOU, Yourself, Outstanding and Unstoppable Today!

Yourself

To be who you truly are on the inside, push past the boundaries of your comfort zone and stretch yourself a little every day.

Dare To Be YOU, Yourself, Outstanding and Unstoppable Today!

Yourself

Being free means you rise so far above the negative things of this world with a loving and selfless heart and not seek revenge for the wrongdoings that have hurt you.

Dare To Be YOU, Yourself, Outstanding and Unstoppable Today!

Yourself

Knowing, loving, and being yourself in life are the most precious gifts you can give to yourself.

Dare To Be YOU, Yourself, Outstanding and Unstoppable Today!

Yourself

Be you
Be all that you are
Be all that you can be
but never be anything less!

Dare To Be YOU, Yourself, Outstanding and Unstoppable Today!

Yourself

When people try to put you down, ignore them, as it's got nothing to do with you and everything to do with what's inside of them.

Dare To Be YOU, Yourself, Outstanding and Unstoppable Today!

Yourself

Let your inner light shine so the entire world can see just how amazing you really are. Never dim that light for anyone or anything!

Dare To Be YOU, Yourself, Outstanding and Unstoppable Today!

Yourself

Do one thing every day that challenges you and the "NORMs" of society and pushes you outside your comfort zone, as true growth is all about this.

Dare To Be YOU, Yourself, Outstanding and Unstoppable Today!

Yourself

Be the best version of yourself that you can be. Don't let others put you down, as their behavior is about them and not you.

Dare To Be YOU, Yourself, Outstanding and Unstoppable Today!

Yourself

Make self care your number one priority because you'll need your health to enjoy your life.

Dare To Be YOU, Yourself, Outstanding and Unstoppable Today!

Yourself

Unless you can and will go deep within yourself for the answers you seek, then you can't say you know and love yourself.

Dare To Be YOU, Yourself, Outstanding and Unstoppable Today!

Yourself

Transformation is a gradual process.
If you want the transformation to be permanent, work on it little by little every day.

Dare To Be YOU, Yourself, Outstanding and Unstoppable Today!

Yourself

I am strong,
I am confident,
I am powerful,
The most important thing is
I've got this!

Dare To Be YOU, Yourself, Outstanding and Unstoppable Today!

Yourself

When you get rejected, remember that this is only a redirection to something far more amazing for you. Rejection brings you so much closer to what you really want and deserve.

Dare To Be YOU, Yourself, Outstanding and Unstoppable Today!

Yourself

It's time to show the world what you are made of by taking your power back, standing firm and tall within your own personal power.

Dare To Be YOU, Yourself, Outstanding and Unstoppable Today!

Yourself

If you don't know how to do something, don't be afraid to step outside your comfort zone. Have a play around to figure it out.
After all, you don't learn through not doing thing.

Dare To Be YOU, Yourself, Outstanding and Unstoppable Today!

Yourself

Failing and making mistakes is the best way to learn and become even better.
Don't be afraid to fail and make mistakes.

Dare To Be YOU, Yourself, Outstanding and Unstoppable Today!

Yourself

When you are the truest version of yourself that you can be, you will always push through the bad stuff and learn the lessons you need to, to get to the good stuff.

Dare To Be YOU, Yourself, Outstanding and Unstoppable Today!

Yourself

You only get one life, so stay healthy, love, laugh lots and stay safe.

Dare To Be YOU, Yourself, Outstanding and Unstoppable Today!

Yourself

Can't is just an excuse for why you won't do something. Having a can do attitude will turn your life around.

Dare To Be YOU, Yourself, Outstanding and Unstoppable Today!

Yourself

You don't have your health; you don't have a life, so put your health first.

Dare To Be YOU, Yourself, Outstanding and Unstoppable Today!

Yourself

Standing up for yourself is the only way to be heard in life about what you want.

Dare To Be YOU, Yourself, Outstanding and Unstoppable Today!

Yourself

Trusting the process isn't easy, but sometimes you need to sit back and let the universe work its magic.

Dare To Be YOU, Yourself, Outstanding and Unstoppable Today!

Yourself

Never feel bad for being an amazing, strong and positive person.
You are who you are and no one but you can change that.
Individuality is a blessing.

Dare To Be YOU, Yourself, Outstanding and Unstoppable Today!

Yourself

When people deceive and lie to you no matter how close they are to you.
You need to remove them from your life.

Dare To Be YOU, Yourself, Outstanding and Unstoppable Today!

Yourself

If you wait for the perfect moment to do things, life will only pass you by.
Do what you need to now and don't hesitate.

Dare To Be YOU, Yourself, Outstanding and Unstoppable Today!

Yourself

There are going to be good and bad days, as that's what life is about.
Please don't let the bad days consume you as there is a light at the end of that tunnel waiting for you.

Dare To Be YOU, Yourself, Outstanding and Unstoppable Today!

Yourself

If you want things to change in your life, then your habits need to change.

Dare To Be YOU, Yourself, Outstanding and Unstoppable Today!

Yourself

Expect nothing and receive a lot.

Dare To Be YOU, Yourself, Outstanding and Unstoppable Today!

Yourself

Your past gives you the strength of character to be who you are now.

Dare To Be YOU, Yourself, Outstanding and Unstoppable Today!

Yourself

When you come to bumps in the road, this doesn't mean you stop.
You just need to go over or around the bumps to continue to your destination.

Dare To Be YOU, Yourself, Outstanding and Unstoppable Today!

Yourself

You can't run from your problems because no matter where you go, you will still be the same person and the problems will follow you.

Dare To Be YOU, Yourself, Outstanding and Unstoppable Today!

Yourself

Nobody knows where life will take us, but what we know is it will be a bumpy ride until we reach the final destination.

Dare To Be YOU, Yourself, Outstanding and Unstoppable Today!

Yourself

Help people because you want to, not because there is a reward in it for you. Seeing the smiles on people's faces should be enough of a reward for you.

Dare To Be YOU, Yourself, Outstanding and Unstoppable Today!

Yourself

Stand in your truth when things get tough and the truth will protect you.

Dare To Be YOU, Yourself, Outstanding and Unstoppable Today!

Yourself

The challenge makes things appealing to do.
If there is no challenge, it wouldn't be worthwhile doing.

Dare To Be YOU, Yourself, Outstanding and Unstoppable Today!

Yourself

Love and live life, but don't take it for granted.

Dare To Be YOU, Yourself, Outstanding and Unstoppable Today!

Yourself

Daring to be you is all about having the courage to stand up for yourself, saying NO to people and the things you don't want to do and meaning it.
Do you Dare To Be You in your life?

Dare To Be YOU, Yourself, Outstanding and Unstoppable Today!

Yourself

Being happy and positive is a choice.
Choose wisely your thoughts, words and actions.

Dare To Be YOU, Yourself, Outstanding and Unstoppable Today!

Yourself

Improving your internal relationship with yourself will help you become 100% more successful in life.

Dare To Be YOU, Yourself, Outstanding and Unstoppable Today!

Yourself

It is amazing what you will find when you search deep within yourself for all your answers. Your soul has the deepest and darkest secrets and it also holds all the answers you seek in life.

Dare To Be YOU, Yourself, Outstanding and Unstoppable Today!

Yourself

Serving others is about using the best parts of yourself and selflessly helping others.

Dare To Be YOU, Yourself, Outstanding and Unstoppable Today!

Yourself

The journey to achieve fulfillment and be truly happy in life happens when you navigate a lot of rocky terrains.
These terrains are along the way to your true destination.

Dare To Be YOU, Yourself, Outstanding and Unstoppable Today!

Yourself

To everything you do, there is a theme.
Look for that theme and figure out if that theme serves you.
If it doesn't, then learn the lessons and change the theme.

Dare To Be YOU, Yourself, Outstanding and Unstoppable Today!

Yourself

You only get one life, so laugh, love, and forgive as much as possible.

Dare To Be YOU, Yourself, Outstanding and Unstoppable Today!

Yourself

Change is uncomfortable with that change comes a new life, but this new life will cost you your old life, which is that comfy place called your comfort zone.

Dare To Be YOU, Yourself, Outstanding and Unstoppable Today!

Yourself

You are awesome, amazing and courageous in your life. Nothing and no one should ever be able to hold you back, so just go for it and see where life takes you.

Dare To Be YOU, Yourself, Outstanding and Unstoppable Today!

Yourself

The future hasn't happened yet.
The past is gone.
The here and now is all we have, so enjoy every moment.

Dare To Be YOU, Yourself, Outstanding and Unstoppable Today!

Yourself

Life is 50% ups and 50% downs
You must always show a balance between the two.

Dare To Be YOU, Yourself, Outstanding and Unstoppable Today!

Yourself

There are those who are realists.
Those who are fake in life.
Those who no matter the battles in life fight, inspire and push to change the "NORMs".
Which are you?

Dare To Be YOU, Yourself, Outstanding and Unstoppable Today!

Yourself

Deciding what can and can't affect you emotionally it isn't easy as we are raised to be negatively geared, but it is possible.

Dare To Be YOU, Yourself, Outstanding and Unstoppable Today!

Yourself

Do something every day that makes your heart sing and make that one thing a part of your daily ritual.

Dare To Be YOU, Yourself, Outstanding and Unstoppable Today!

Yourself

Self–belief is missing in society today.
Instead of challenging the "NORMs" we seem to be afraid of judgement.
To grow, one must always challenge ourselves and the "NORMs" and have self–belief.

Dare To Be YOU, Yourself, Outstanding and Unstoppable Today!

Yourself

When things get rough, there is no point getting grumpy or stroppy.
You just need to weather the storm and move forward positively.

Dare To Be YOU, Yourself, Outstanding and Unstoppable Today!

Yourself

You can be courageously comfortable in stretching yourself past your comfort zone.
It won't be easy.
So make getting outside your comfort zone a habit in your life.

Dare To Be YOU, Yourself, Outstanding and Unstoppable Today!

Yourself

I am no longer hiding my true self from others.
By hiding behind the mask of pretending to be what everyone wants me to be for their approval, as this is betraying me.
The only approval I need is my own.

Dare To Be YOU, Yourself, Outstanding and Unstoppable Today!

Yourself

When the way is dark, list all the good things you have in your life and meditate on them. This will give you that guiding light you need to keep going.

Dare To Be YOU, Yourself, Outstanding and Unstoppable Today!

Yourself

Never stop learning because knowledge gives you power.
The moment you stop, you lose that power.
Use that power wisely.

Dare To Be YOU, Yourself, Outstanding and Unstoppable Today!

Yourself

Being busy does not mean that you neglect your health, as you are the one consistent thing in your life.
If you don't have your health, you can't enjoy your life.

Dare To Be YOU, Yourself, Outstanding and Unstoppable Today!

Yourself

You should not be ashamed of failing and making mistakes, as that is the best way to learn and to become even better.

Dare To Be YOU, Yourself, Outstanding and Unstoppable Today!

Yourself

When you are your truest version of yourself that you can be, you can and will always push through all the bad stuff to get to the good stuff and learn the lessons you need to.

Dare To Be YOU, Yourself, Outstanding and Unstoppable Today!

Yourself

With self-love and self-belief, you will never go searching for or need the approval of others, as you know deep down inside that you are enough.

Dare To Be YOU, Yourself, Outstanding and Unstoppable Today!

Yourself

People will only see what they want to see, so why waste time worrying about what they think of you?
What matters is what you think about yourself.

Dare To Be YOU, Yourself, Outstanding and Unstoppable Today!

Yourself

Don't change for others, change for yourself, as that is where true and everlasting transformation happens.

Dare To Be YOU, Yourself, Outstanding and Unstoppable Today!

Yourself

What price do you put on your own personal progress and growth?
It should be infinite, as you should put yourself first, no matter what.

Dare To Be YOU, Yourself, Outstanding and Unstoppable Today!

Yourself

There is no such thing as perfect.
Near enough is good enough.
What matters most is that you get things done.
You've got this!

Dare To Be YOU, Yourself, Outstanding and Unstoppable Today!

Yourself

Your life is a gift, so why not be grateful and appreciate it by looking after yourself holistically?
If you don't have your health, what do you have?

Dare To Be YOU, Yourself, Outstanding and Unstoppable Today!

Yourself

Removing the ego makes you the truest version of yourself that you can be.

Dare To Be YOU, Yourself, Outstanding and Unstoppable Today!

Yourself

When you believe in yourself, you will realize you are far smarter, competent, and capable than you think you are.

Dare To Be YOU, Yourself, Outstanding and Unstoppable Today!

Yourself

It's okay to relax and to have down time as you need to do what's best for you.
Only you know what you need.

Dare To Be YOU, Yourself, Outstanding and Unstoppable Today!

Yourself

No matter how much someone tries to bring you down because they feel threatened and insecure around you, don't let them win.
Have confidence that you are better than they are.

Dare To Be YOU, Yourself, Outstanding and Unstoppable Today!

Yourself

Searching in life for something that is not there will only lead you down a rabbit hole full of sadness and discomfort.
Stop searching and be grateful for the things you have.

Dare To Be YOU, Yourself, Outstanding and Unstoppable Today!

Yourself

Instead of challenging the "NORMs" we seem to be afraid of Judgement.
To grow, one must always challenge things, be curious and believe in oneself.

Dare To Be YOU, Yourself, Outstanding and Unstoppable Today!

Yourself

Do not let other people's opinions of you affect how you feel about yourself. Their opinions say more about them than they do about you.

Dare To Be YOU, Yourself, Outstanding and Unstoppable Today!

Yourself

Bullies and narcissists project their insecurities onto others to make themselves feel good.
If this is happening to you, it has nothing to do with you.
It is their power play.

Dare To Be YOU, Yourself, Outstanding and Unstoppable Today!

Yourself

Knowing your big why (what motivates and moves you forward) is important, as it will help you overcome obstacles.

Dare To Be YOU, Yourself, Outstanding and Unstoppable Today!

Yourself

You will be at peace when you totally accept who you are and what can and can't be changed in life.

Dare To Be YOU, Yourself, Outstanding and Unstoppable Today!

Yourself

Never apologize for being the person you are.
Either people will love you or they will hate you, but it's their choice either way.

Dare To Be YOU, Yourself, Outstanding and Unstoppable Today!

Yourself

Good people are everywhere.
You just need to know how to attract them into your life, and that's the hard part.

Dare To Be YOU, Yourself, Outstanding and Unstoppable Today!

Yourself

Before judging someone, remember that we've all been through different things, so put on their shoes and try to understand them first.

Dare To Be YOU, Yourself, Outstanding and Unstoppable Today!

Yourself

When you figure out who the most important person is in your life, all the pieces will fall into place.

Dare To Be YOU, Yourself, Outstanding and Unstoppable Today!

Yourself

Self-love and self-belief are the two most powerful things on the planet.
Once you have these two things, you can, with a little discipline, reach the stars.

Dare To Be YOU, Yourself, Outstanding and Unstoppable Today!

Yourself

To be happy, love yourself fully first.
Then you can love others and they can love you unconditionally.

Dare To Be YOU, Yourself, Outstanding and Unstoppable Today!

Yourself

It's important to be the truest version of yourself you can be.
Never pretend to be someone else for the approval of others.

Dare To Be YOU, Yourself, Outstanding and Unstoppable Today!

Yourself

The most precious gift you can give yourself is knowing, loving, and being yourself in life.

Dare To Be YOU, Yourself, Outstanding and Unstoppable Today!

Yourself

I am Strong.
I am Quirky.
I am Talented.
I am Unique.
I am an Original.
I love who I am.

Dare To Be YOU, Yourself, Outstanding and Unstoppable Today!

Yourself

Today I vow to nurture, love and to always respect myself. I vow to speak and stand in my truth at all times.

Dare To Be YOU, Yourself, Outstanding and Unstoppable Today!

Yourself

If you want other people to believe in you and do what needs to be done by change, make the change first and be the example.

Dare To Be YOU, Yourself, Outstanding and Unstoppable Today!

Yourself

Be you and all that you are. Show the world that even through the darkest times, you will shine brightly to help others and yourself find the way.

Dare To Be YOU, Yourself, Outstanding and Unstoppable Today!

Yourself

People are at one point or another going to let you down.
Know that you are worth more than that and never let it get you down. Simply move on.

Dare To Be YOU, Yourself, Outstanding and Unstoppable Today!

Yourself

Your choices in life make you who you truly are.
If you don't take responsibility for your choices, you are destined for a life of repeats.

Dare To Be YOU, Yourself, Outstanding and Unstoppable Today!

Yourself

You don't have to be annoying or obnoxious to use your voice and share your truths.
All you need to be is yourself and the wonderful person you are.

Dare To Be YOU, Yourself, Outstanding and Unstoppable Today!

Yourself

Be the very best version of yourself that you can be. Don't let others diminish who you are.

Dare To Be YOU, Yourself, Outstanding and Unstoppable Today!

Yourself

Quit worrying about what other people think of you and worry about what you think of yourself.
Don't change for others change for yourself.

Dare To Be YOU, Yourself, Outstanding and Unstoppable Today!

Yourself

Other people fake their lives on social media to gain approval from others and to get new clients in.
I choose to show the good and the bad and how I have overcome the bad to help others improve their lives.

Dare To Be YOU, Yourself, Outstanding and Unstoppable Today!

Yourself

Being a realist is far better than being someone who fakes it until you make it, as you are honest with yourself and others and you earn their respect and aren't seen as a lair.

Dare To Be YOU, Yourself, Outstanding and Unstoppable Today!

Yourself

Having the courage and belief in yourself to stand up and speak your truth even though you have a fear of judgement & of not being enough is empowering.
So why not try it?

Dare To Be YOU, Yourself, Outstanding and Unstoppable Today!

Yourself

What is the price you put on your own personal progress and growth?
It should be infinite, as you should put yourself first, no matter what.

Dare To Be YOU, Yourself, Outstanding and Unstoppable Today!

Yourself

The silent confidence in women is bold, strong, courageous and sexy.

Dare To Be YOU, Yourself, Outstanding and Unstoppable Today!

Yourself

Change only for yourself and not because other people want you to.
Self love, acceptance and respect mean more than other people's approval.

Dare To Be YOU, Yourself, Outstanding and Unstoppable Today!

Yourself

Let your soul shine through because when you do this, you will never lose your way, even through the roughest of storms.

Dare To Be YOU, Yourself, Outstanding and Unstoppable Today!

Yourself

Your destiny is not written in stone.
You can change direction, do something new to alter your path at anytime.
All it takes is a change in mindset.

Dare To Be YOU, Yourself, Outstanding and Unstoppable Today!

Yourself

Never let other people tell you that you have too high standards and that you should lower them.
Your standards are there to protect you.

Dare To Be YOU, Yourself, Outstanding and Unstoppable Today!

Yourself

Healing is a slow process, so stop being so hard on yourself and ease up on yourself.
Always take the full time to recover.
Your holistic health matters.

Dare To Be YOU, Yourself, Outstanding and Unstoppable Today!

Yourself

No matter how driven for success you are, don't lose sight of your own health.

Dare To Be YOU, Yourself, Outstanding and Unstoppable Today!

Yourself

I am strong,
I am quirky,
I am unique,
I am an original,
I love who I am.

Dare To Be YOU, Yourself,
Outstanding and Unstoppable
Today!

Yourself

Remember to be YOU,
with a can DO attitude
and you will go far in life.

Dare To Be YOU, Yourself, Outstanding and Unstoppable Today!

Yourself

I am confident,
I am courageous,
I am brave, and I am fearless.
I experience all life offers me and yet I am not myself, as I wear a thousand masks to please others.
This is changing as of now!

Dare To Be YOU, Yourself, Outstanding and Unstoppable Today!

Yourself

Little by little, a caterpillar transforms into a beautiful butterfly and breaks out of its comfort zone.
It never evolves without complete trust in the transformation process that the transformation can happen.

Dare To Be YOU, Yourself, Outstanding and Unstoppable Today!

Yourself

Life is not a given, it is a gift, so be grateful for it. Never take it for granted.

Dare To Be YOU, Yourself, Outstanding and Unstoppable Today!

Yourself

You are loved and
supported by the universe,
no matter what.
So, stop hiding behind your
excuses and start living your
life authentically.

Dare To Be YOU, Yourself,
Outstanding and Unstoppable
Today!

Yourself

Life is what you want it to be. If you choose to believe the negative and suspect everything, then that's what you will attract.
Stay positive and real and your life will be positive and real.

Dare To Be YOU, Yourself, Outstanding and Unstoppable Today!

Yourself

Reflect on your life and how far you've come today when things get you down.
You are amazing in every way.

Dare To Be YOU, Yourself, Outstanding and Unstoppable Today!

Yourself

Don't react to life respond to life.

Dare To Be YOU, Yourself, Outstanding and Unstoppable Today!

Yourself

Never bring your own personal baggage from unresolved past issues into your work or other relationships, as it can cause irreparable damage.

Dare To Be YOU, Yourself, Outstanding and Unstoppable Today!

Yourself

Always remember to laugh, relax and enjoy your life because you never know when you may have to be serious again.

Dare To Be YOU, Yourself, Outstanding and Unstoppable Today!

Yourself

You are stronger, smarter, more fun, more interesting than you think you are, so don't let others tell you otherwise.

Dare To Be YOU, Yourself, Outstanding and Unstoppable Today!

Yourself

I am special,
I am interesting,
I am abundantly prosperous
in all things.

Dare To Be YOU, Yourself,
Outstanding and Unstoppable
Today!

Yourself

It is absolutely necessary to cut toxic people out of your life.
They do way more harm than good staying in your life.

Dare To Be YOU, Yourself, Outstanding and Unstoppable Today!

Yourself

When life gets you down, keep going as you don't know what wonderfully exciting things await you.

Dare To Be YOU, Yourself, Outstanding and Unstoppable Today!

Yourself

Your life changes forever when you know your worth and can speak and stand in your truth.

Dare To Be YOU, Yourself, Outstanding and Unstoppable Today!

Yourself

Abundance flows easily and quickly into my life now.

Dare To Be YOU, Yourself, Outstanding and Unstoppable Today!

Yourself

Let the universe guide you through life and just go with it.

Dare To Be YOU, Yourself, Outstanding and Unstoppable Today!

Yourself

When stuck in your head, bring yourself back to your heart space by taking some deep breaths in and out and meditating for a while.
Your heart space is the place of service.

Dare To Be YOU, Yourself, Outstanding and Unstoppable Today!

Yourself

When you focus on the positives in life, miracles will happen.

Dare To Be YOU, Yourself, Outstanding and Unstoppable Today!

Yourself

When things get you down, change your focus.
Focus on all the positives in your life.

Dare To Be YOU, Yourself, Outstanding and Unstoppable Today!

Yourself

When using the written and spoken language, use them wisely as people will read into things what they will, according to their own experiences.

Dare To Be YOU, Yourself, Outstanding and Unstoppable Today!

Yourself

We all have struggles with who we are from time to time because we live in a world of societal stereotyping and constraints.
In these times, look within yourself to find out who you really are.

Dare To Be YOU, Yourself, Outstanding and Unstoppable Today!

Yourself

Your heart will always steer you in the right direction, so always listen to it.

Dare To Be YOU, Yourself, Outstanding and Unstoppable Today!

Yourself

Through great adversity comes significant possibility and hope.

Dare To Be YOU, Yourself, Outstanding and Unstoppable Today!

Yourself

Listen to your body when it says it needs rest, as running yourself into the ground won't do you any good.

Dare To Be YOU, Yourself, Outstanding and Unstoppable Today!

Yourself

STOP rushing to get things done.
Take a breath and relax for a while to recover.
Not everything needs to be done immediately.

Dare To Be YOU, Yourself,
Outstanding and Unstoppable Today!

Yourself

You are not doing things right if you don't have haters and trolls, trolling through your posts and commenting on errors and nitpicking your posts.

Dare To Be YOU, Yourself, Outstanding and Unstoppable Today!

Yourself

Never let the views of someone who doesn't know you or your life try to tell you what's happening in your life or how you should feel about it.

Dare To Be YOU, Yourself, Outstanding and Unstoppable Today!

Yourself

Loving yourself is always being honest with yourself and keeping the promises you make to yourself.

Dare To Be YOU, Yourself, Outstanding and Unstoppable Today!

Yourself

All the answers you seek are within you, so dig deep within yourself and you will find them.

Dare To Be YOU, Yourself, Outstanding and Unstoppable Today!

Yourself

Your thoughts, actions, reactions, and emotions are all that you can control. Everything outside of yourself you can't control, so why blame yourself for other people's wrongdoings?

Dare To Be YOU, Yourself, Outstanding and Unstoppable Today!

Yourself

When difficult situations arise, always remember to be the best version of yourself you can be.

Dare To Be YOU, Yourself, Outstanding and Unstoppable Today!

Yourself

Tomorrow is not guaranteed and not to be taken for granted.
Live each day like it's your last, as you never know what's around the corner.

Dare To Be YOU, Yourself, Outstanding and Unstoppable Today!

Yourself

You are amazing just the way you are.
Don't let the societal "NORMS" and stereotypes change the person you really are.

Dare To Be YOU, Yourself, Outstanding and Unstoppable Today!

Yourself

There is no physical dollar value to my personal worth, so today I vow to love, honor, and protect myself.

Dare To Be YOU, Yourself, Outstanding and Unstoppable Today!

Yourself

You know you are on the path to success when you have social media haters and copycats.
Always know that you are the only original.

Dare To Be YOU, Yourself, Outstanding and Unstoppable Today!

Yourself

True magic happens when you believe, respect, and love yourself completely and unconditionally.

Dare To Be YOU, Yourself, Outstanding and Unstoppable Today!

Yourself

Stress is a killer, so do all you can to stay relaxed and calm.

Dare To Be YOU, Yourself,
Outstanding and Unstoppable
Today!

Yourself

Holistically speaking, your health should always be your number one priority. Without your health, you can not enjoy your life.

Dare To Be YOU, Yourself, Outstanding and Unstoppable Today!

Yourself

Always be kind and thoughtful to everyone, even those that are disrespectful and unkind to you.
This will show people you vibrate on a higher level.

Dare To Be YOU, Yourself, Outstanding and Unstoppable Today!

Yourself

I am not who I think I am.
I am not who I think you think I am.
I am not who you I think I am.
I am who I know I am, which is far deeper than surface level.

Dare To Be YOU, Yourself, Outstanding and Unstoppable Today!

Yourself

Never let people tell you that you have to disown your past to heal.
You can heal and help others heal through sharing your past.

Dare To Be YOU, Yourself, Outstanding and Unstoppable Today!

Yourself

HOW TO CONTACT ME

Please reach out to me via the following methods if you would like to enquire about anything you have read that may help you in your life's journey or to find out about how my coaching can help you.

https://www.instagram.com/daretobeyoucoaching/

https://www.facebook.com/daretobeyou.net.au

https://www.linkedin.com/company/dare-to-b-you/

https://www.linkedin.com/showcase/daretobyou/

https://daretobeyou.net.au/contact-get-in-touch

https://www.youtube.com/@Dare.To.Be.You.

https://twitter.com/DiehmLynette

SIGN UP FOR A FREE DARE TO BE YOU - GRATITUDE DIARY

Click the link below to be redirected to my website, where you can download your FREE copy of your gratitude diary. Take that first step to helping you!

Click here to download for free!

Go to: https://daretobeyou.net.au to download the Dare To Be You–Gratitude Diary **NOW!**

REVIEWS

Enjoy this book? You can make a big difference

Reviews are the most powerful tools in my arsenal for getting attention for my books. As much as I'd like to, I don't have the financial muscle of a New York publisher. I can't take out full-page ads in the newspaper or put posters on the subway. (not yet anyway).

But I have something much more powerful and effective than that, and it's something those publishers would kill to get their hands on.

A committed and loyal bunch of readers

Honest reviews of my books help bring them to the attention of other readers. If you've enjoyed this book, I would be very grateful if you could spend just five minutes leaving a review (it can be as short as you like) on Goodreads or the Amazon the book's sales page. I'd be extremely grateful.

Thank you.

AUTHOR'S NOTE

I'd like to thank you for reading this book and I trust you have gained some valuable tools to start your days off on a positive note. I wrote this book to inspire and give you the tools you need to move you positively forward past the roadblocks that may come up in your life.

www.ingramcontent.com/pod-product-compliance
Lightning Source LLC
Chambersburg PA
CBHW060504090426
42735CB00011B/2110